# POEMS FOR SPRING

## Selected by
## Robert Hull

## Illustrated by
## Annabel Spenceley

STECK-VAUGHN
L I B R A R Y
A Division of Steck-Vaughn Company

*Austin, Texas*

# Seasonal Poetry

## Poems for Autumn
## Poems for Spring
## Poems for Summer
## Poems for Winter

Series editor: Catherine Ellis
Designer: Ross George

**Library of Congress Cataloging in Publication Data**
Poems for spring / selected by Robert Hull : illustrated by Annabel
Spenceley
  p. cm. — (Seasonal poetry)
  Includes index.
  Summary: An anthology of poems reflecting spring by such authors
as Elizabeth Coatsworth, Emily Dickinson, Langston Hughes, and
Rudyard Kipling
  ISBN 0-8114-7802-5
  1. Spring — Juvenile poetry. 2. Children's poetry. 3. Poetry —
Collections.  4. English poetry — Translations from foreign
languages. [1. Spring — Poetry.  2. Poetry — Collections.]
I. Hull, Robert.  II. Spenceley, Annabel. ill.  III. Series.
PN6109.97.P635 1991
808.81'933 — dc20                90-20592
                            CIP AC

## Picture Acknowledgments
The publishers would like to thank the
following for allowing their illustrations to be
reproduced in this book: Ardea *Cover*, Bruce
Coleman 7 (Hans Reinhard), 10 (Sinielsen),
13 (Hans Reinhard), 16 (B. & C Alexander),
20 (Andy Purcell), 27 (Eric Crichton), 34 (Dr
Eckart Pott), 38 (Kim Taylor), 43 (P.A.
Hinchliffe); the Hutchison Library 37; Oxford
Scientific Films 24 (Steve Littlewood), 28
(Raymond Blythe), 40 (Stephen Dalton), 48
(Jos Korenromp); ZEFA 5, 8, 15, 19, 23, 31, 32.

Typeset by Nicola Taylor, Wayland
Printed in Italy by G. Canale & C.S.p.A.
Bound in the United States.
1  2  3  4  5  Ca  95  94  93  92  91

## Acknowledgments
For permission to reprint copyright material
the publishers gratefully acknowledge the
following: Penguin Books Ltd for three haiku
by Yosa Buson, from *The Penguin Book of
Japanese Verse*, translated by Geoffrey
Bownas and Anthony Thwaite (Penguin,
1964, translation copyright © Geoffrey
Bownas and Anthony Thwaite, 1964);
Macmillan Publishing Company for "March"
from *Summer Green* by Elizabeth
Coatsworth. Copyright 1948 by Macmillan
Publishing Company, renewed 1976 by
Elizabeth Coatsworth Beston; Paul Coltman
for "Snowdrops"; "Bee! I'm expecting you"
reprinted by permission of the publishers
and the Trustees of Amherst College from
*The Poems of Emily Dickinson* edited by
Thomas H. Johnson, Cambridge, Mass.: The
Belknap Press of Harvard University Press,
copyright 1951, © 1955, 1979, 1983 by the
President and Fellows of Harvard College;
the Estate of Robert Frost, the editor and
Jonathan Cape Ltd for "Spring Pools" from
*The Poetry of Robert Frost* edited by Edward
Connery Lathem; "April Rain Song" from *The
Dreamkeeper and Other Poems* by Langston
Hughes, reprinted by permission of the
author and David Higham Associates Ltd; in
the USA copyright 1932 by Alfred A. Knopf,
Inc. and renewed 1960 by Langston Hughes.
Reprinted by permission of Alfred A. Knopf,
Inc; Artisjus, Budapest for "The Birth of the
Foal" by Ferdinand Juhász; the author and
Harrap Publishing Group Ltd for "Crows"
from *Mr Bidery's Spidery Garden* by David
McCord; "At long last, spring has arrived"
and "I planted some seeds" by Colin
McNaughton from *There's an Awful Lot of
Weirdos in our Neighbourhood* copyright ©
1987 Colin McNaughton. Published in the UK
by Walker Books Ltd; Irene Rawnsley for
"Time to Dust the Daffodils"; "Bug Spots"
from *Good Morning, America* by Carl
Sandburg, copyright 1928 by Harcourt Brace
Jovanovich, Inc. and renewed 1956 by Carl
Sandburg. Reprinted by permission of the
publisher. While every effort has been made
to trace the copyright holders, in some cases
it has proved impossible. The publishers
apologize for this apparent negligence.

# Contents

# Introduction

"The frogs got home last week," Emily Dickinson says in one of the poems in this book. I know what she means, because about thirty come back every February to our small pond. It's like a busy swimming pool. Spring is risky. One poem in this book tells the story of young foxes who are left motherless. In another a girl hopes her seeds will grow. In another crows shriek at an owl out hunting by day. But it's exciting too. Even for his computer, nine-year-old Gary Lewis says, spring is all "ring ding" and "ding a ling" and "fling spring." For someone's gran it's time to get out the . . . well, have a look and see. And for someone else – I wonder where – it's birds' nest and tadpoles in October.

So what is spring for you? Is it the things these poets have written about – snowdrops that "ring the February winds," pewits that "sport and cry," seeds, rain, puddles and pools, the birth of a young animal, two lovers out walking (if you can find them) – or is it other things? Tell us. Tell us by writing some spring poems.

# *Snowdrops*

On the cold lip of the year
we find them, when the wind
knifes through the thin hedge
and a little fitful light
shrinks before nightfall.

And always they surprise us –
arrive too early and suffer all
winter can whip at them.
Pale flowers. Their blind white eyes
will never see April, but
their bells ring the February winds
untroubled by hope.

**PAUL COLTMAN**

# *At Long Last, Spring Has Arrived!*

At long last, spring has arrived.
"So there you are!" I said icily.
"About time too!" I said frostily.
"You're late!" I said coldly.

"Cool it," she said mildly.
"I've been under a lot of pressure lately.
Have a daffodil."

"Blooming cheek," I said,
In the heat of the moment.

**COLIN McNAUGHTON**

*cheek* – boldness.

# *March*

A blue day,
a blue jay
and a good beginning.

One crow,
melting snow –
spring's winning!

**ELIZABETH COATSWORTH**

# *Crows*

I like to walk
And hear the black crows talk.

I like to lie
And watch crows sail the sky.

I like the crow
That wants the wind to blow:

I like the one
That thinks the wind is fun.

I like to see
Crows spilling from a tree,

And try to find
The top crow left behind.

I like to hear
Crows caw that spring is near.

I like the great
Wild clamor of crow hate

Three farms away
When owls are out by day.

I like the slow
Tired homeward-flying crow;

I like the sight
Of crows for my good night.

**DAVID McCORD**

# *Spring Pools*

These pools that, though in forests, still reflect
The total sky almost without defect,
And like the flowers beside them, chill and shiver,
Will like the flowers beside them soon be gone,
And yet not out by any brook or river,
But up by roots to bring dark foliage on.

The trees that have it in their pent-up buds
To darken nature and be summer woods –
Let them think twice before they use their powers
To blot out and drink up and sweep away
These flowery waters and these watery flowers
From snow that melted only yesterday.

**ROBERT FROST**

# Spring Fjord

I was out in my kayak
I was out at sea in it
I was paddling
very gently in the fjord Ammassivik
there was ice in the water
and on the water a petrel
turned his head this way that way
didn't see me paddling
Suddenly nothing but his tail
then nothing
He plunged but not for me:
huge head upon the water
great hairy seal
giant head with giant eyes, moustache
all shining and dripping
and the seal came gently toward me
Why didn't I harpoon him?
Was I sorry for him?
was it the day, the spring day, the seal
playing in the sun
like me?

**TRADITIONAL INUIT SONG**

*petrel* – a small seabird with long wings.

17

# *Four Little Foxes*

Speak gently, Spring, and make no sudden sound;
For in my windy valley, yesterday I found
New-born foxes squirming on the ground –
          Speak gently.

Walk softly, March, forbear the bitter blow;
Her feet within a trap, her blood upon the snow,
The four little foxes saw their mother go –
          Walk softly.

Go lightly, Spring, oh, give them no alarm;
When I covered them with boughs to shelter them from harm,
The thin blue foxes suckled at my arm –
          Go lightly.

Step softly, March, with your rampant hurricane;
Nuzzling one another, and whimpering with pain,
The new little foxes are shivering in the rain –
          Step softly.

**LEW SARETT**

19

# Spring

As my eyes
search
the prairie
I feel the summer
in the spring.

**CHIPPEWA POEM**
(Translated by F. Densmore)

# Clearing at Dawn

The fields are chill, the sparse rain has stopped;
The colors of Spring teem on every side.
With leaping fish the blue pond is full;
With singing thrushes the green boughs droop.
The flowers of the field have dabbled their powdered cheeks;
The mountain grasses are bent level at the waist.
By the bamboo stream the last fragment of cloud
Blown by the wind slowly scatters away.

**LI PO** (Translated from the Chinese by Arthur Waley)

# *Bug Spots*

This bug carries spots on his back.
Last summer he carried these spots.
Now it is spring and he is back here again
With a domino design over his wings.
All winter he has been in a bedroom,
In a hole, in a hammock, hung up, stuck away,
Stashed while the snow blew over
The wind and the dripping icicles,
The tunnels of the frost.
Now he has errands again in a rotten stump.

**CARL SANDBURG**

# From *In Springtime*

I am sick of endless sunshine, sick of blossom-burdened
    bough.
Give me back the leafless woodlands where the winds of
    Springtime range –
Give me back one day in England, for it's Spring in England
    now!

Through the pines the gusts are booming, o'er the brown
    fields blowing chill,
From the furrow of the plowshare streams the fragrance of
    the loam,
And the hawk nests on the cliffside and the jackdaw in the hill,
And my heart is back in England 'mid the sights and sounds
    of Home.
But the garland of the sacrifice this wealth of rose and peach is
Ah! *koïl*, little *koïl*, singing on the *siris* bough,
In my ears the knell of exile your ceaseless bell like speech
    is –
Can you tell me aught of England or of Spring in England
    now?

**RUDYARD KIPLING**

25

# *Time to Dust the Daffodils*

My gran's too old
to go out
in the cold garden
planting bulbs,
but she likes
spring flowers.

She has a box
of plastic daffodils
on sticks
that she hides away
in the winter.

When she notices
that spring is coming
she takes them out,
dusts each one carefully,

then plants them
underneath her window.

Passers-by pause
to admire them.
"How lovely, Mrs. Paradine!
Why do your daffodils
always bloom earlier
than mine?"

**IRENE RAWNSLEY**

# *Mallee in October*

When clear October suns unfold
mallee tips of red and gold,

children on their way to school
discover tadpoles in a pool,

iceplants sheathed in beaded glass,
spider orchids and shivery grass,

webs with globes of dew alight,
budgerigars on their first flight,

tottery lambs and a stilty foal,
a papery slough that a snake shed whole,

and a bronzewing's nest of twigs so few
that both the sky and the eggs show through.

**W. FLEXMORE HUDSON**

*budgerigars* – a small Australian parrot.
October is spring in Australia.

*mallee* – a low Australian shrub.

29

# *April Rain Song*

Let the rain kiss you.
Let the rain beat upon your head with silver liquid drops.
Let the rain sing you a lullaby.

The rain makes still pools on the sidewalk.
The rain makes running pools in the gutter.
The rain plays a little sleep-song on our roof at night –

And I love the rain.

**LANGSTON HUGHES**

# I Planted Some Seeds

I planted some seeds
In my garden today.
They haven't come up yet,
I hope they're okay.

Should I dig them all up,
Take them back to the shop?
Ask for my money back,
Say they're a flop?

Perhaps they were faulty,
Perhaps they were duff,
Maybe they haven't
Been watered enough.

I planted some seeds
In my garden today.
They haven't come up yet,
I hope they're okay.

**COLIN McNAUGHTON**

*duff* – slang for something worthless or useless.

# *The Flower-Fed Buffaloes*

The flower-fed buffaloes of the spring
In the days of long ago,
Ranged where the locomotives sing
And the prairie flowers lie low –
The tossing, blooming, perfumed grass
Is swept away by the wheat,
Wheels and wheels and wheels spin by
In the spring that still is sweet.
But the flower-fed buffaloes of the spring
Left us, long ago.
They gore no more, they bellow no more,
They trundle around the hills no more –
With the Blackfeet, lying low,
With the Pawnees, lying low,
Lying low.

**VACHEL LINDSAY**

35

# *Spring Haiku*

Spring rain:
Telling a tale as they go,
Straw cape, umbrella.

———

Sudden shower:
Grasping the grass-blades
A shoal of sparrows.

———

Spring rain;
Soaking on the roof
A child's rag ball.

**YOSA BUSON**

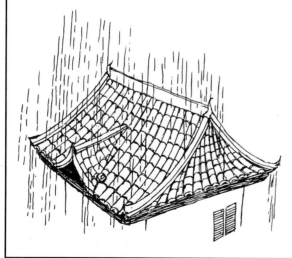

*shoal* – a crowd.

# *Bee! I'm Expecting You!*

Bee! I'm expecting you!
Was saying Yesterday
To Somebody you know
That you were due –

The Frogs got Home last Week –
Are settled, and at work –
Birds, mostly back –
The Clover warm and thick –

You'll get my Letter by
The seventeenth; Reply
Or better, be with me –
Yours, Fly.

**EMILY DICKINSON**

# *The Computer's Spring Greeting*

Spring gling
flingle jingle
jing wring
sing wing
bring ting
ring ding
dingle ding
ding a ling
ling a ring
ring ring
jing a ring
wing a ling
spring a ling
spring swing
wing ing
fling spring
sprang spring
SPR. . . . . . .ING!
SPRING

**GARY LEWIS (Age 9)**

# *Two Pewits*

Under the after-sunset sky
Two pewits sport and cry,
More white than is the moon on high
Riding the dark surge silently;
More black than earth. Their cry
Is the one sound under the sky.
They alone move, now low, now high,
And merrily they cry
To the mischievous Spring sky,
Plunging earthward, tossing high,
Over the ghost who wonders why
So merrily they cry and fly,
Nor choose 'twixt earth and sky,
While the moon's quarter silently
Rides, and earth rests as silently.

**EDWARD THOMAS**

*pewit* – a bird with a narrow crest.

# *Birth of the Foal*

As May was opening the rosebuds,
elder and lilac beginning to bloom,
it was time for the mare to foal.
She'd rest herself, or hobble lazily

after the boy who sang as he led her
to pasture, wading through the meadowflowers.
They wandered back at dusk, bone-tired,
the moon perched on a blue shoulder of sky.

Then the mare lay down,
sweating and trembling, on her straw in the stable.
The drowsy, heavy-bellied cows
surrounded her, waiting, watching, snuffing.

Later, when even the hay slept
and the shaft of the Plow pointed south,
the foal was born. Hours the mare
spent licking the foal with its glue-blind eyes.

And the foal slept at her side,
a heap of feathers ripped from a bed.
Straw never spread as soft as this.
Milk or snow never slept as soft as a foal.

*the Plow* – a constellation, also known as the Big Dipper.

Dawn bounced up in a bright red hat,
waved at the world and skipped away.
Up staggered the foal,
its hooves were jelly-knots of foam.

Then day sniffed with its blue nose
through the open stable window, and found them –
the foal nuzzling its mother,
velvet fumbling for her milk.

Then all the trees were talking at once,
chickens scrabbled in the yard,
like golden flowers
envy withered the last stars.

**FERENC JUHÁSZ**

45

# Biographies

**Yosa Buson** (1715–83) was famous as a painter and writer of haiku, the 3-line poem that has been popular in Japan for centuries. He wrote more than 2,000 haiku.

**Elizabeth Coatsworth** was born in Buffalo, New York, in 1893. She traveled a great deal even as a child, and later wrote poems for adults and children. Her most popular book for children is called *The Cat Who Went to Heaven*.

**Paul Coltman** lives in Sussex, England. He has two collections of poems for adults, and two books for children, the very well-known *Tog the Ribber* and *Witch Watch* – both with illustrations by his daughter, Gillian McClure. A third children's book, *Tinker Jim*, will be published soon.

**Emily Dickinson** (1830–1886) was one of the greatest American poets. She lived a basically reclusive life in her family's Amherst, Massachusetts, home writing poetry. Only seven of her poems were published during her lifetime. Six volumes of poetry were published after her death. She could say a great deal in a few short lines.

**Robert Frost** (1874–1963) is one of the most famous American poets of this century. He was born in California, and later lived on a farm in New Hampshire. Though he did not write especially for children, many of his poems are children's favorites.

**W. Flexmore Hudson** was born in Queensland, Australia, in 1913. He was a teacher and a seaman as well as a writer of several books of poetry. He wrote about the Australian countryside in all its moods; his best-known work, *Drought*, is about the harsh side of life in the Mallee country.

**Langston Hughes** (1902–67) has written stories, plays, and novels, as well as several books of poems. He is especially remembered for capturing in his writing the experience of African-Americans in the U.S.

**Ferenc Juhász** is a Hungarian writer, who was born in 1928 in Bia, a village near Budapest, where he now lives. When he was only 22 he won the highest poetry prize in Hungary.

**Rudyard Kipling** was born in Bombay in 1865. He worked as a journalist and wrote his first poems and stories for newspapers and for the Indian Railway Library. He wrote many stories for children. After leaving India, he lived in Vermont, and then in Sussex, England, where he died in 1936. He was the first English writer to receive the Nobel Prize.

**Li Po** (701–761) was one of the greatest Chinese poets. He was born near present-day Afghanistan, and his family went to China when he was about five. He spent much of his time wandering, and is supposed to have died by falling out of a boat, trying to "embrace the moon in the river."

**Vachel Lindsay** (1879–1931) was born in Springfield, Illinois. He studied art at college, then decided to be "a tramp and a beggar," wandering around the country, getting food and a bed in exchange for reading and performing his poems.

**David McCord**, an American poet, was born in 1897. He has written books about many things – art, education, medicine, and history – but he is best known for his light verse, and especially his poems for children.

**Colin McNaughton** studied illustration at the Royal College of Art, London. He illustrated many books for children before starting to write children's verse, and soon had a book published called *There's an Awful Lot of Weirdos in our Neighbourhood.*

**Irene Rawnsley** lives in Settle, Yorkshire, England. In 1988 Methuen published a collection of her poems for children called *Ask a Silly Question*, and a second book, *Dog's Dinner*, in 1990.

**Carl Sandburg** was an American writer who lived from 1878 to 1967. After leaving school he wandered around the Mid-West, then went to fight in the Spanish-American war. He wrote many stories and poems for children, which are collected in *The Sandburg Treasury.*

**Lew Sarett** (1888–1954) was born in Chicago, and lived most of his life in the Rocky Mountains and northern Canada. He wrote several books of poems about those places, and about the life of the native Americans.

**Edward Thomas** (1878–1917) wrote many books, but we remember him most for his poetry, written toward the end of his life. He was killed in 1917 in Flanders, during World War I, at the age of 38.

# Index of First Lines

First published in 1990 by
Wayland (Publishers) Ltd

© Copyright 1990 Wayland
(Publishers) Ltd